MW01514574

HEARING
GOD

HOW ORDINARY PEOPLE HEAR GOD'S VOICE

RICHARD EXLEY

WORD & SPIRIT
PUBLISHING

Give us ears to hear Your voice

and a heart to receive Your Word.

Give us the will to obey

and the faith to act.

Amen.

Unless otherwise indicated, all Scripture quotations are taken from the Holy Bible, New International Version®, NIV®. Copyright © 1973, 1978, 1984, 2011 by Biblica, Inc.TM Used by permission of Zondervan. All rights reserved worldwide. www.zondervan.com. The "NIV" and "New International Version" are trademarks registered in the United States Patent and Trademark Office by Biblica, Inc.™

Scripture quotations marked MSG are taken from The Message. Copyright © 1993, 2002, 2018 by Eugene H. Peterson.

Scripture quotations marked NLT are taken from the Holy Bible, New Living Translation, copyright © 1996, 2004, 2015 by Tyndale House Foundation. Used by permission of Tyndale House Publishers, Inc., Carol Stream, Illinois 60188. All rights reserved.

Scripture quotations marked NKJV are taken from the New King James Version®. Copyright © 1982 by Thomas Nelson. Used by permission. All rights reserved.

Scripture quotations marked KJV are taken from the King James Version of the Bible. Public domain.

Hearing God
How Ordinary People Hear God's Voice
Copyright © 2021 by Richard Exley
ISBN: 978-1-949106-56-5

Published by Word and Spirit Publishing
P.O. Box 701403
Tulsa, Oklahoma 74170
wordandspiritpublishing.com

Printed in the United States of America. All rights reserved under International Copyright Law. Content and/or cover may not be reproduced in whole or in part in any form without the expressed written consent of the Publisher.

CONTENTS

CHAPTER 1

RECOGNIZING GOD'S VOICE

For God speaks again and again, though people do not recognize it. He speaks in dreams, in visions of the night, when deep sleep falls on people as they lie in their beds. He whispers in their ears and terrifies them with warnings. He makes them turn from doing wrong; he keeps them from pride.

JOB 33:14–17 NLT

The biblical record is clear—God wants to communicate with us. According to Job, "God speaks again and again" (Job 33:14 NLT). That being the case, why do so many of us feel like He seldom, if ever, speaks to us personally? Could it be that we are not listening? Or maybe we have mistakenly concluded that while God spoke to people during biblical times, He no longer speaks to ordinary people like you and me.

I beg to differ. I concur with Frederick William Fabian, who writes, "There is hardly ever a complete silence in our soul. God is whispering to us well nigh incessantly . . . only we do not always hear because of the noise, hurry, and distraction which life causes as it rushes on."

And maybe it is not just the noise of the world that makes us deaf to the voice of God. Maybe we simply do not recognize His voice.

So how does He speak to us? What does His voice sound like?

Based on both Scripture and experience, I would like to suggest that God speaks to us in one of three or four ways, or some combination thereof. The most common way the Lord speaks to us is through the Bible—His divinely inspired Word. It is also the plumb line by which we judge every other "word" we receive. If a word does not line up with Scripture, we must reject it.

The second way the Lord speaks to us is through the prompting of the Holy Spirit. Paul says, "The Spirit itself beareth witness with our spirit" (Romans 8:16 KJV). We sometimes call this the "still, small voice," alluding to Elijah's experience on Mount Horeb (1 Kings 19:11–13 KJV).

The third way He speaks to us is through godly people. For instance, Scripture tells us that as Paul was sailing to Rome, "the weather was becoming dangerous for sea travel because it was so late in the fall, and **Paul spoke to the ship's officers about it.** 'Men,' he said, 'I believe there is trouble ahead if we go on—shipwreck, loss of cargo, and danger to our lives as well.' But the officer in charge of the prisoners listened more to the ship's captain and the owner than to Paul" (Acts 27:9–11 NLT, emphasis mine).

Although God was speaking through Paul to warn the men in the ship, they refused to take heed. As a result, they were caught in a savage storm and shipwrecked.

The fourth way the Lord speaks is through mystical experiences, like dreams, visions, and prophecy. For example, "During the night Paul had a vision of a man of Macedonia standing and begging him, 'Come over to Macedonia and help us.' After Paul had seen the vision, we got ready at once to leave for Macedonia, concluding that God

had called us to preach the gospel to them."
(Acts 16:9–10).

In Acts 21, Paul received a prophetic
word from a prophet named Agabus. He
"took Paul's belt, tied his own hands and feet
with it and said, 'The Holy Spirit says, "In
this way the Jewish leaders in Jerusalem will
bind the owner of this belt and will hand him
over to the Gentiles."'" (Acts 21:11).

To this point, I have used only scrip-
tural examples to illustrate how God speaks
to us. I have done this deliberately, in order
to establish a solid biblical foundation. In
the coming chapters, I will share numerous
examples of God speaking to people just like
you and me.

A word of caution—don't strain to hear
God's voice. If you do, you will likely imagine
He is speaking when He is not. Instead, simply
live in quiet expectancy, paying attention to

the thoughts and impressions that come to you, "for God does speak—now one way, now another" (Job 33:14).

CHAPTER 2

HEARING GOD'S VOICE THROUGH THE SCRIPTURES

Jesus answered, "It is written: 'Man shall not live on bread alone, but on every word that comes from the mouth of God.'"

MATTHEW 4:4

God speaks to us most often through the Bible. It is unique. It is unlike any other book known to man. Many different writers, separated by hundreds of years and living in diverse places, wrote it under the inspiration of the Holy Spirit. It contains sixty-six books—thirty-nine in the Old Testament and twenty-seven in the New Testament—yet it has a common theme, a thread that ties it all together.

It reveals who God is and who He has created us to be. It is the revelation of His character, the declaration of His plans and purposes in our world, the proclamation of His law, and the Good News of His mercy and grace! It shows the way of salvation and reveals God's plan for our lives. Psalm 139 declares, "You saw me before I was born. Every day of my life was recorded in your book. Every moment was laid out before a single day had passed. How precious are your thoughts about me, O God" (Psalm 139:16–17 NLT).

The Ten Commandments declare God's moral law. Proverbs provides wisdom and insight for living. The historical books and the Prophets reveal God's presence in history. The Gospels tell the story of Jesus' earthly ministry, His death, and His resurrection. All of this is critically important if we are to discern God's will and live a life pleasing to the Lord.

I am told that in the Library of Congress there is a copy of the Constitution, which, when viewed from a certain angle, bears the likeness of George Washington, the father of our country. So it is with the Scriptures. When we come to them through faith, we see the heart of God. He reveals Himself to us through His Word.

So, what do the eternal Scriptures tell us about God?

James says there's not even a shadow of turning or variableness in His character (James 1:17). In other words, you don't have to worry about what kind of "mood"

God will be in when you come to Him. He is the same yesterday, today, and forever (Hebrews 13:8).

God loves us unconditionally—He always has and always will! "But God demonstrates his own love for us in this: While we were still sinners, Christ died for us" (Romans 5:8). Speaking through the prophet Jeremiah, the Lord said, "I've never quit loving you and never will. Expect love, love, and more love!" (Jeremiah 31:3 MSG).

He is a gracious heavenly Father who knows what we need even before we ask (Matthew 6:8). It is His pleasure to give us the Kingdom (Luke 12:32), and He invites us to "come boldly to the throne of grace" and make our needs known (Hebrews 4:16 NKJV). He promises to supply all of our needs through His riches in Christ Jesus (Philippians 4:19). And He is able to do abundantly more than we could ever ask or even imagine (Ephesians 3:20).

When we are tempted, He is faithful to make a way of escape (1 Corinthians 10:13). If we sin, He is faithful and just to forgive our sins and cleanse us from all unrighteousness (1 John 1:9). And He is "a very present help in trouble" (Psalm 46:1 NKJV).

I concur with Frank Gaebelein, who counsels, "Maintain at all costs a daily time of Scripture reading and prayer. As I look back, I see that the most formative influence in my life and thought has been my daily contact with Scripture over sixty years."

If you truly desire to hear God's voice, live in the Word! Read it. Study it. Meditate upon it. Memorize it. Hide it in your heart, and in your darkest hour, you will hear His voice, and it will sustain you.

CHAPTER 3

HEARING GOD'S VOICE THROUGH THE SCRIPTURES, PART 2

All Scripture is inspired by God and is useful to teach us what is true and to make us realize what is wrong in our lives. It corrects us when we are wrong and teaches us to do what is right.

2 TIMOTHY 3:16 NLT

We do not need a special spiritual experience to hear the Lord speak to us through

His Word. Every time we read the Scriptures or meditate on them, He is speaking to us. However, there may be special occasions when He "highlights" a particular Scripture exactly when we need it. Maybe you've had an experience like that. Many believers have.

Several years ago, a young woman was going through an unspeakably difficult time. In desperation, she took her Bible and crawled into the bathroom, where she collapsed on the floor in tears. Never had she felt so alone. Not only had her husband been unfaithful, but others she trusted had betrayed her as well. For what seemed like a long time, she sobbed bitterly, crying out to the Lord, but it seemed the heavens were brass. No matter how hard she tried, she could not sense God's presence or hear His voice.

Picking up her tear-dampened Bible, she hugged it to her chest. "Lord Jesus," she prayed, "I have to have a word from You or I will die."

Although she knew it was not a wise practice, she closed her eyes and opened her Bible randomly. Blindly she jabbed her finger on the page. Through her tears, she read, "Though you have made me see troubles, many and bitter, **you will restore my life again . . . . You will increase my honor and comfort me once more**" (Psalm 71:20–21, emphasis mine).

The hope and assurance that verse brought her could not have been any greater had the Lord spoken to her in an audible voice. Grabbing a ballpoint pen and several 3 X 5 index cards, she began copying those verses. When she had made several copies, she placed them in strategic places—on her makeup mirror, on the nightstand beside her bed, on the refrigerator door, on the visor in her car, and in her purse.

Although she continued to battle grief and depression, she no longer felt totally alone. When circumstances threatened to overwhelm her, she returned to Psalm 71: ". . . You [God] will restore my life again . . . . You will increase my honor and comfort me once more."

God doesn't always speak in that way. In fact, it is the exception rather than the rule, but it happens frequently enough to convince me that the Lord will do whatever is necessary to get our attention.

At other times, you may simply be reading the Word when a verse of Scripture seems to leap off the page. In that moment, you know the Lord has a personal word for you through that particular verse. Sometimes it is a warning to keep you from making a poor decision or yielding to temptation. At other times, it is a word of direction or a word of comfort or assurance.

When I was going through a particularly difficult time, the Lord spoke to me from Psalm 138. After an amazing period of growth, the congregation I was serving seemed to plateau. To make matters worse, my latest book was not selling nearly as well as anticipated. Consequently, I was struggling with doubts regarding my effectiveness and my future ministry.

My Bible-reading schedule took me to Psalm 138. When I came to verses 7 and 8, they seemed to leap off the page: "Though I walk in the midst of trouble, you preserve my life. You stretch out your hand against the anger of my foes; with your right hand you save me. **The LORD will fulfill, his purpose, for me**" (Psalm 138:7–8, emphasis mine).

The circumstances that were so troubling didn't immediately change. There was no sudden surge in attendance or book sales, but I was no longer anxious. God had spoken to me through His Word. My future was in His hands, and He promised to fulfill His purpose in my life!

Spending time with the Lord is the key. Open the Scriptures and linger over them in His presence. As you wait before the Lord, let the Word speak to you. Let it strengthen and encourage you. For instance, Psalm 121:7–8 says, "The LORD will keep you from all harm—he will watch over your life; the LORD will watch over your coming and going both now and forevermore."

That's His word to you!

CHAPTER 4

HEARING GOD'S VOICE THROUGH THE PROMPTING OF THE HOLY SPIRIT

Meanwhile, as Peter was puzzling over the vision, the Holy Spirit said to him, "Three men have come looking for you. Get up, go downstairs, and go with them without hesitation. Don't worry, for I have sent them."

ACTS 10:19–20 NLT

Let me say it again: The most frequent way the Lord speaks to us is through the Bible—His divinely inspired Word. It is also the plumb line by which we judge every other "word" we receive. If it does not line up with Scripture, we must reject it. Having reemphasized that, let me share another common way the Lord speaks to ordinary people like you and me.

We sense, or "feel impressed," that we should do or not do a certain thing. It is both a feeling and a thought. As we pay attention to that "feeling," it becomes clearer in our minds. Of course, we examine the Scriptures to make sure that what we are feeling lines up with the Word. If it does, we move forward in obedience.

During the last days of the Great Depression, Reverend Bill Mitchell sensed the Lord directing him to go to Craig, Colorado. Those were difficult times, and Craig was four hundred miles away. It didn't seem to make any sense, but he couldn't escape the feeling that the Lord was directing him.

The more he thought and prayed about it, the clearer his impressions became. Now a street address sprang full-blown into his mind, and he felt the Lord "tell" him that a young woman who lived at that address was praying for a preacher to come to Craig and start an Assemblies of God church.

As he was trying to decide if he was truly hearing from the Lord, or if his imagination was simply running away with him, he was reminded of Philip's experience in Acts 8. An angel of the Lord directed Philip to "go south to the road . . . that goes down from Jerusalem to Gaza" (Acts 8:26). When he got there, he encountered an Ethiopian official and "the Spirit told Philip, 'Go to that chariot and stay near it'" (Acts 8:29). Because Philip heard and obeyed the voice of the Spirit, the Ethiopian official was saved and baptized (Acts 8:38).

Although Bill was encouraged, he still had doubts. How could he be sure the Lord was truly directing him? As he thought and prayed about it, he asked himself if this was the kind of thing the Lord would do. Based on Philip's experience in Acts 8 and Peter's experience in Acts 10, he concluded that it was.

He was still unsure, so he continued to examine his feelings, asking himself several questions: Did he have any reason or desire to go to Craig? No. Had he ever thought about going to Craig to start a church? Never. Since there was a biblical precedent, and since he had absolutely no personal reason to go to Craig, he concluded the Lord was directing him.

It was midmorning when he arrived at the address the Lord had "impressed" upon his mind. Taking a deep breath, he breathed a prayer and then knocked on the door. When a young man answered the door, he introduced himself saying, "I'm Bill Mitchell from Lamar, Colorado. The Lord directed me to this address. He said a young woman who lived here was praying for a preacher to come to Craig and start an Assemblies of God church."

The young woman who was praying was Eleanor Phillips, my father's oldest sister. That very evening, Bill Mitchell held the first service in that small house, and Eleanor's backslidden husband, who had ridiculed her for praying, recommitted his life to the Lord and was called to preach. In the months ahead, Bill Mitchell pioneered the Craig Assembly of God. My father, who was still in high school, helped him build the first church building. Nearly forty years later, the congregation of the Craig Assembly of God called Brenda and me to serve as their pastors.

The way the Lord "spoke" to Reverend Bill Mitchell is not uncommon. He often speaks to ordinary people like you and me in the same way. **Bill did not hear an audible voice, but rather he had an impression, or a "feeling," that became a thought.** As he thought and prayed about it, the "feeling" became stronger, and he received more details.

According to David Wilkerson, "The will of God grows on you. That which is of God will fasten itself on you and overpower and possess your entire being. That which is not of God will die—you will lose interest. But the plan of God will never die. The thing God wants you to do will become stronger each day in your thoughts, in your prayers, in your planning. It grows and grows!"[1]

You may be thinking, *That's all well and good, but nothing like that ever happens to me.* You may even be tempted to think that God would never speak to you. You're not a preacher, or anyone special, so why would He speak to you? Or you may think you're too spiritually deaf to hear His voice even if He did speak to you. Don't be discouraged; even if you have never heard Him speak, you can learn to hear and recognize His voice.

CHAPTER 5

HEARING GOD'S VOICE THROUGH THE PROMPTING OF THE HOLY SPIRIT, PART 2

A third time the LORD called, "Samuel!" And Samuel got up and went to Eli and said, "Here I am; you called me." Then Eli realized that the LORD was calling the boy. So Eli told Samuel, "Go and lie down, and if he calls you, say, 'Speak, LORD, for your servant is listening.'"

1 SAMUEL 3:8–9

Following the Wednesday night Bible study, a young man made his way across the parking lot toward his car. The pastor had taught about listening to God and obeying His voice, and he could not help but wonder, "Does God really speak to ordinary people like me?"

Sitting in his car, he prayed, "God, if You still speak to people, speak to me. I will listen. I will do my best to obey." Of course, he didn't hear anything, but as he drove out of the parking lot, he had the strangest thought. *Stop and buy a gallon of milk.*

He shook his head and said out loud, "God, is that You?" He didn't get a reply, and so he continued driving. But again, the thought came, *Buy a gallon of milk.*

He decided it didn't seem like too hard a test of obedience. Even if it was just his imagination and not God's voice, he could always use the milk, so he stopped and purchased a gallon of milk.

Back in the car, he headed for home. As he passed Seventh Street, he again felt an urge, *Turn down that street.*

This is crazy, he thought and drove on past the intersection. Again, he felt the prompting to turn down Seventh Street, so at the next intersection, he turned around and headed down Seventh.

He drove several blocks, when suddenly, he felt prompted to stop. Pulling over to the curb, he looked around. He was in a semi-commercial area of town. It wasn't the best neighborhood, but it wasn't the worst, either. The businesses were closed, and most of the houses were dark.

Again, a thought sprang into his mind, *Give the milk to the people in the house across the street.*

The house was dark, and it looked like whoever lived there was either gone or already in bed. Still, he opened the car door and started to get out, and then he hesitated. "Lord," he said, "this is insane. If those people are home, they are probably asleep. If I wake them, they're going to be mad."

Closing the door, he started the car and prepared to drive off. Suddenly, he was nearly overwhelmed with a feeling that the Lord was disappointed with him. Reluctantly, he turned the car off and opened the door. "Okay, God," he said, "I will give them the milk even if they think I'm some kind of nut. I want to be obedient."

When he rang the doorbell, he heard a man holler, "Who is it? What do you want?"

Feeling uncomfortable, he started to set the milk on the porch and leave. Just then the door opened, and he found himself face-to-face with a man dressed in jeans and a T-shirt. "What is it?" the man demanded.

Not knowing what to say, he simply thrust the gallon of milk at him. "Here, I brought this to you." For just an instant, the man stared at him in disbelief, and then he took the milk and rushed down the hallway. Almost immediately, a woman appeared, carrying the milk toward the kitchen. Right behind her came the man, holding a crying baby.

Over his shoulder he said, "We had some unexpected expenses this month, and we ran out of money. We didn't have any milk for our baby. We were just praying and asking God to show us how to get some milk when you knocked on the door."

His wife yelled from the kitchen. "I asked God to send an angel with milk for our baby. Are you an angel?"

That young man was hardly an angel. What he was, was a sincere believer who hungered to hear God's voice. And not just to hear it, but also to obey. And because he was obedient to the Lord's prompting, a young couple's desperate prayer was answered!

The Lord seldom speaks simply to satisfy our curiosity. Rather, His word comes as marching orders to the committed. According to Hannah Whitall Smith, "The way in which the Holy Spirit, therefore, usually works, in a fully obedient soul, in regard to this direct guidance, is to impress upon the mind a wish or desire to do or to leave undone certain things."[2]

Let me encourage you to pay attention to the thoughts and impressions that come to you, for that is often how the Lord speaks. If what you are sensing lines up with Scripture, act on it, even if you are not sure whether it is God's voice or just your imagination. That's what Abraham did: "By faith Abraham, when called to go to a place he would later receive as his inheritance, obeyed and went, even though he did not know where he was going" (Hebrew 11:8).

CHAPTER 6

HEARING GOD'S VOICE THROUGH GODLY PEOPLE

Then he taught me, and he said to me, "Take hold of my words with all your heart; keep my commands, and you will live. Get wisdom, get understanding; do not forget my words or turn away from them. Do not forsake wisdom, and she will protect you; love her, and she will watch over you.

PROVERBS 4:4–6

May I remind you that the Lord usually speaks to us in one of three or four ways, or in some combination thereof? Thus far, we have considered how He speaks to us through Scripture and through the prompting of the Holy Spirit. The Spirit's prompting usually comes to us as a feeling, which becomes a conscious thought, impressing us to do, or not to do, a certain thing.

Now we turn our attention to how He speaks to us through others. Sometimes His words come to us through an anointed sermon or while we are reading a book filled with spiritual truth. At other times, the Lord may speak to us when we seek the advice of a counselor or a spiritual friend. He may even speak to us through a friend during an ordinary conversation.

I'm thinking of a man who married a widow who had already buried two husbands. Knowing how he grieved when his wife of more than fifty years passed, he asked her how she did it. How did she go on living after losing two husbands to death? She replied, "Life goes on, if you let it." That was all, but in that moment, he realized the Lord was giving him the key to move beyond his grief. It was his wife's words and her voice, but it was the Lord who spoke to him.

Think about it. You've probably had experiences like that, even if you did not realize the Lord was speaking to you until later. Sometimes we don't recognize the significance of something that was said until we have had time to think about it. If it's truly a word from the Lord, we will find ourselves returning to it again and again, especially during our quiet times. As we prayerfully consider the insights we received, we will realize that God Himself was speaking to us.

For instance, when I was a young preacher, I made some foolish mistakes.

In the aftermath, I grew depressed, and I wondered if God still loved me. In the wee hours of the morning, I found myself alone in the living room and unable to sleep. "God," I prayed, "do You love me?" At that very moment, my eighteen-month-old daughter pulled herself up on the couch and straddled my chest. Putting her chubby hands on my tear-damp cheeks, she said, "Luv you, Daddy. Luv you."

It was her voice I heard, but it was the Lord who spoke to me as surely as He spoke to Jeremiah hundreds of years ago: "I've never quit loving you and never will. Expect love, love, and more love!" (Jeremiah 31:3 MSG).

Some years ago, a ministerial colleague was trying to determine the will of the Lord regarding an important decision. Denominational officials had offered him the leadership position of an international ministry. Although he was deeply fulfilled in his current ministry, he was intrigued by the opportunity to lead an international ministry, not to mention being tempted by the status that would come with it.

He did not want to make a mistake and miss the will of God, so he prayed and fasted, he searched the Scriptures, he discussed it with his wife, and he sought the counsel of trusted colleagues. Still, he wasn't sure what he should do.

Several weeks passed, and the denominational officials were pressing him for a decision. One morning, the telephone rang in his office. When he answered it, there was a moment of silence, then an embarrassed explanation. The caller explained that he had intended to telephone someone else and had inadvertently hit the wrong speed-dial button. "Sorry," he apologized, "I called the wrong man."

After hanging up the telephone, my colleague had his answer. He had heard the voice of the Lord in the words spoken by a colleague who had called him by mistake. He sensed in his spirit that the denominational officials had simply "called the wrong man."

What about you? Have you ever had a similar experience? Have there been times when the Lord spoke to you through the words of a friend or a counselor? Have you applied them to your life, or have you simply forgotten them? Maybe you didn't realize the Lord was speaking to you, or perhaps you simply didn't want to hear it. It doesn't matter. The Lord still wants to speak to you.

Put your finger between the pages of this little book and reflect on the thoughts and feelings you are experiencing. Replay some of the recent conversations you have had with spiritually mature believers. If nothing comes to mind, don't try to force it. Just determine that in the future you will be alert for those moments when the Lord speaks, however His "word" may come to you.

CHAPTER 7

HEARING GOD'S VOICE THROUGH GODLY PEOPLE, PART 2

That night Paul had a vision: A man from Macedonia in northern Greece was standing there, pleading with him, "Come over to Macedonia and help us!" So we decided to leave for Macedonia at once, having concluded that God was calling us to preach the Good News there.

ACTS 16:9–10 NLT

If your current position is deeply fulfilling and you have two elementary-age children, the last thing you want to do is resign your position, uproot your family, and relocate to another country. That's the situation in which Don and Melba found themselves. They had been serving as church-planting missionaries in Argentina for nearly seven years. With the Lord's help, they had planted several churches, and they had no thoughts of going anywhere. With an effective ministry and a host of friends, they were deeply fulfilled.

All of that changed at the Southern Cone Missionary Retreat, when Loren Triplett, the regional director for Latin America, presented the Mexico City vision—to plant churches in the world's largest city. For Don and Melba, listening to Loren was akin to Paul hearing the man from Macedonia pleading with him, "Come over to Macedonia and help us!" (Acts 16:9 NLT). The voice was

Loren Triplett's, but it was the Holy Spirit who was speaking to them.

They were both deeply committed to the will of the Lord, but this simply did not make sense. If they uprooted their family and moved to Mexico City for one year, they would be turning their back on nearly eight years of ministry in Argentina. After a year in Mexico City, they would be required to return to the United States for an additional year of itineration before they could return to Argentina. It didn't seem to make any sense, yet they sensed the Lord directing them.

For several weeks, they wrestled with the Lord. It was a huge decision, and they didn't want to make a mistake. Nonetheless, the more they prayed and thought about it, the more convinced they were that the Lord was calling them to Mexico City. It was nearly killing Melba. She didn't want to be disobedient to the Lord, and she didn't want to hold

Don back if this was what the Lord was calling them to do, but she had to be certain. Before making a final decision, Don decided to fly to Lima, Peru, to meet with Loren Triplett to finalize plans to be part of the Mexico City task force. If the Lord was truly directing them to Mexico City, Loren would agree to their change of countries and confirm their desire to become part of the team.

Although Melba trusted Don's spiritual leadership, on a decision this big, she also had to hear from the Lord for herself. With Don gone to Peru and the children in school, she had some time to wait before the Lord. After weeping and praying for a considerable length of time, she still wasn't certain regarding the Lord's direction. That particular day, her Bible reading schedule took her to 1 Kings 19. When she read verse 7, it was like the Lord Himself spoke to her: "Get up and eat, for the journey is too much for you."

Instantly she knew it was the Lord's way of telling her that He was sending them to Mexico City, but not to fear. Although the "journey" was too much for her, she knew the Lord was telling her that He would take care of her and their children. The challenges of relocating to another country were still daunting, but she was at peace. The Lord had spoken! Likewise, Don's meeting with Loren Triplett confirmed the Lord's call.

When they arrived in Mexico City, they learned they would be the only church planters in that great city of twenty-three million people, as a number of unforeseen circumstances had prevented any other members of the task force from joining them. In spite of working alone, the Lord helped them purchase property and build a ministry team that would make up the future pastoral staff for the new congregation. At the end of their year in Mexico City, they turned over a thriving congregation of approximately two hundred converts to the new pastors. In the ensuing years, the church has flourished. They built a one-thousand-seat sanctuary, launched a Christian school, and planted several other churches in Mexico.

I share Don and Melba's experience because it illustrates how the Lord speaks to us in a combination of ways. First, He spoke to Don and Melba through Loren's sermon. It was like the Lord Himself was speaking to both of them. Then He continued to press His call upon their hearts by the prompting of the Holy Spirit. Finally, He used the Scriptures to confirm His direction to Melba, while He used Loren Triplett to confirm what Don was feeling in his spirit.

You may be thinking that you're not a missionary, so how does this relate to you? Psalm 37:23 says, "The LORD directs the steps of the godly. He delights in every detail of their lives" (NLT). It doesn't say the Lord only directs the steps of a missionary or a pastor, but that He directs the steps of the godly. He delights in every detail of your life, and He wants to direct your steps. He may speak to you through the Scriptures, or through the prompting of your spirit, or through another person, or some combination thereof.

I challenge you to surrender unconditionally to the Lord and ask Him to speak to you. Now get ready—"For God does speak—now one way, now another" (Job 33:14).

CHAPTER 8

HEARING GOD'S VOICE THROUGH DREAMS

*"'In the last days, God says, I will pour out my Spirit on all people. Your sons and daughters will prophesy, your young men will see visions, **your old men will dream dreams.** Even on my servants, both men and women, I will pour out my Spirit in those days, and they will prophesy.'"*

ACTS 2:17–18, emphasis mine

Many people mistakenly assume God only speaks to special individuals and only on special occasions. That's simply not the case. Of course, any time the Lord speaks to us is special, but it is neither rare nor unique. Every time we open the Bible, God speaks to us through His Word. During our quiet times, He often communicates with us through thoughts and impressions. Sometimes He even speaks to us through other people. These are the "ordinary" ways in which He communicates with us. Now I want to consider one of the more mystical or supernatural ways He speaks—through dreams.

One of the first questions people ask is, "How do I know if my dream is truly from the Lord, or if I ate too much pizza before going to bed?" That's a great question. The only criteria the Bible gives for determining the validity of our dreams is the "Word" test. If it doesn't line up with the Scriptures, your dream is not from the Lord.

I'm thinking of a man who dreamed he was supposed to marry a certain woman. The only problem was that the woman was already married. Nonetheless, he was absolutely convinced his dream was from the Lord. I told him his dream couldn't be from the Lord because it violated Scripture. I then quoted Deuteronomy 5:18, 21: "You shall not commit adultery," and "You shall not covet your neighbor's wife."

Even if your dream passes the "Word" test, that doesn't necessarily mean it is from the Lord. Most of us dream virtually every night. I know I do, and most of my dreams are simply nonsensical. When I awaken, I usually can't remember them in detail, and I don't give them a second thought. But when God gives me a dream, it is clear. When I awaken, the details are imprinted on my memory, and I immediately sense that the dream was from the Lord. If it is truly from the Lord, it will grow stronger as you wait. If it is not from the Lord, it will fade.

Dreaming the same dream repeatedly is another indication it may be a "God" dream. For instance, at least once a month for nearly ten years, I dreamed I was called to serve a church in crisis. The church never had a name or a location, but it was always in crisis. After dreaming that dream several times, I became convinced that at some future date, a church in crisis would call and ask us to become their pastor. In March 2010, we were called to Gateway Church in Shreveport, Louisiana. They were in a serious crisis. Had the Lord not prepared me through those dreams, I might have been hesitant to accept the call to serve as their pastor.

In my experience, our dreams often deal with issues in our own life. On several occasions, the Lord used my dreams to convict

me and sanctify me. Through a series of
three dreams—one of which I dreamt several
times—He dealt with my anger, my ego,
and my ambition. Although the dreams
were excruciatingly painful, the healing they
produced was truly liberating.

At other times, the Lord may use dreams
to warn us of impending danger. Consider
this entry from my journal dated Monday,
April 23, 1986:

*I dreamed that I was kidnapped by terror-
ists while flying to Africa. They were holding
me prisoner in the international airport in
Copenhagen, Denmark. Eventually the mili-
tary rescued me, but the last thing one of the
terrorists said to me was, "You've escaped
this time, but when you come to Lowa, we
will kill you." I had never heard of Lowa, so
I looked in a 1986 World Atlas and the only
Lowa in the world was in Zaire, Africa.*

That same night, an evangelist who ministers in the office of a prophet received two visions warning me not to go to Africa, and a lady in our church dreamed a dream in which the Lord spoke to her saying, "Tell your pastor not to go to Africa."

As I pondered those dreams, I couldn't help but think of Joseph, the earthly father of Jesus. In a dream, the Lord told him to, "take the child and his mother and escape to Egypt. Stay there until I tell you, for Herod is going to search for the child to kill him" (Matthew 2:13).

Twice more, the Lord warned Joseph in dreams regarding the safety of Jesus. Matthew 2:19–20 tells us: "After Herod died, **an angel of the Lord appeared in a dream to Joseph** in Egypt and said, 'Get up, take the child and his mother and go to the land of Israel, for those who were trying to take the child's life are dead'" (emphasis mine). And in verse

22: "When [Joseph] heard that Archelaus was reigning in Judea in place of his father Herod, he was afraid to go there. **Having been warned in a dream,** he withdrew to the district of Galilee" (emphasis mine).

Needless to say, I heeded the warning the Lord gave me through dreams and canceled my trip to Africa.

What can we conclude from an overview of the Scriptures regarding dreams? Just this, dreams were a common way the Lord spoke to people in biblical times, and every person who received a dream from the Lord took it seriously. The Bible doesn't tell us how they knew their dreams were from God, but the way they responded is proof they were convinced their dreams were authentic. In some cases, they were even willing to risk their lives in obedience to their God-given dreams.

Let me say it again—don't strain to hear God's voice. If you do, you will likely imagine He is speaking when He is not. This is especially true when it comes to dreams. If God wants to speak to you through a dream, He will, and when He does, you will know it.

CHAPTER 9

HEARING GOD'S VOICE THROUGH VISIONS

*"'In the last days, God says, I will pour out my Spirit on all people. Your sons and daughters will prophesy, **your young men will see visions,** your old men will dream dreams. Even on my servants, both men and women, I will pour out my Spirit in those days, and they will prophesy.'"*

ACTS 2:17–18, emphasis mine

Like dreams, visions have a predominant place in Scripture.[3] But unlike dreams, which are a common experience, seeing an open vision is fairly rare. Dreams occur when we are sleeping, while visions come to us when we are wide awake. Other than that, seeing a vision is very much like dreaming a God-given dream.

It's important to note that the Lord never gives an open vision without a purpose. When He appeared to Ananias in a vision, His purpose was to restore Saul's sight and commission him as a missionary to the Gentiles (see Acts 9:10–18). When the angel of the Lord appeared to Cornelius in a vision, the Lord's purpose was to open the door for the Holy Spirit to be poured out on the Gentiles (see Acts 10). When Paul received a vision in which a man of Macedonia was begging him, "Come over to Macedonia and help us," God's purpose couldn't have been clearer. Luke says, "After Paul had seen the vision, we got ready at once to leave for Macedonia, **concluding that God had called us to preach the gospel to them**" (Acts 16:10, emphasis mine).

An open vision also gives special assurance to the recipient when his mission is especially risky. I hardly think Ananias would have had the courage to lay hands on Saul if the Lord hadn't called to him in an open vision. He knew of Saul's reputation for zealously persecuting the followers of Christ (Acts 9:1–2), and he was hesitant to risk confronting him. Acts 9 puts it this way, "In Damascus there was a disciple named Ananias. **The Lord called to him in a vision . . .** 'Lord,' Ananias answered, 'I have heard many reports about this man and all the harm he has done to your holy people in Jerusalem. And he has come here with authority from the chief priests to arrest all who call on your name.' But the Lord said to Ananias, 'Go! This man is my chosen instrument to proclaim my name to the Gentiles and their kings and to the people of Israel. . . .' Then Ananias went . . ." (Acts 9:10, 13-15, 17, emphasis mine).

I sincerely doubt Peter would have risked the misunderstanding of his peers by going to the home of an uncircumcised Gentile if the Lord hadn't given him an open vision in which He told him, "Do not call anything impure that God has made clean" (Acts 10:15). Then the Spirit said to him, "Simon, three men are looking for you. . . . Do not hesitate to go with them, for I have sent them" (Acts 10:19–20). As a result of Peter's obedience, the Holy Spirit was poured out on the Gentiles (Acts 10:44–48).

No sincere believer doubts that the Lord spoke to people through visions in New Testament times. The biblical record is clear. The question is, Does God still speak to people through visions in the twenty-first century?

Let me respond with an emphatic "Yes!" Acts 2:17 declares, "'**In the last days,** God says, I will pour out my Spirit on all people. Your sons and daughters will prophesy, **your young men will see visions,** your old men will dream dreams'" (emphasis mine).

In the spring of 1985, the Lord gave me an open vision. In my vision, I was standing in the middle of the construction debris in Christian Chapel's unfinished auditorium. As I watched, I saw a man pushing a wheelbarrow. I followed him as he made his way into a small prayer room off the platform. When he emptied his wheelbarrow, I suddenly realized it was filled with money. Back in the unfinished auditorium, I noticed there were green exit lights over the doors exiting the auditorium. As I was focusing on them, the Holy Spirit spoke to me, "When the exit lights go up, the man with the wheelbarrow will make a delivery."

That vision was critical because we were nearing completion on our new auditorium, and we were somewhere between forty and fifty thousand dollars short of having the necessary funds to pay the final construction invoice. Had I not received that vision, I would have been under a great deal of pressure to find a way to raise the needed funds. Instead of feeling pressured, I was at peace.

Each morning, before going down the hall to my office, I opened the door to the auditorium to see if the exit lights had been installed. Day after day I was disappointed, and several weeks went by before I finally saw the electricians installing them. Initially I was ecstatic, but about halfway to my office, I had a paralyzing thought. *What if the man with the wheelbarrow doesn't make a delivery?* Now I castigated myself. *Why had I shared my vision with the congregation? What was I thinking?*

By the time I reached my office, I was sick with worry. I couldn't help wondering if that vision had really happened, or if it was just a figment of my imagination.

My first appointment was with a medical student. After introducing herself, she said, "My great-grandmother passed away some months ago, and she left me one hundred thousand dollars. The check arrived yesterday, and the Lord told me to give the tithe to Christian Chapel." Opening her purse, she took out a check for ten thousand dollars and handed it to me. Two days later, a businessman came to my office and gave me a $33,000 check made out to Christian Chapel.

Amazing! The very day the exit lights were installed, the "man with the wheelbarrow" made a delivery, just like the Lord had said he would.

I once thought that if I ever had an open vision, I would never question its authenticity.

Boy, was I wrong! During the course of my lifetime, the Lord has only given me two open visions, and both times I couldn't help thinking, *Did that really happen, or was it just my imagination?* I can only conclude that however God speaks to us, it will require faith to receive His message and faith to act on it.

CHAPTER 10

HEARING GOD'S VOICE THROUGH PROPHECY

*Even on my servants, both men and women, I will pour out my Spirit in those days, **and they will prophesy.***

ACTS 2:18, emphasis mine

*A spiritual gift is given to each of us so we can help each other. . . . He gives one person the power to perform miracles, **and another the ability to prophesy.***

1 CORINTHIANS 12:7, 10 NLT, emphasis mine

Although prophecy was common in both the Old and New Testament,[4] it is perhaps the most controversial and misunderstood way the Lord speaks to us. It is one of the spiritual gifts listed in 1 Corinthians 12, and its purpose is to strengthen, encourage, and comfort those who hear it. For instance, "Judas and Silas, who themselves were prophets, said much to encourage and strengthen the believers" in Antioch (Acts 15:32).

I must confess that initially I was very skeptical of prophecy. Why? Several reasons: 1) I was largely unaware of what the Scriptures had to say on the subject. 2) Most of the people who exercised this gift seemed strange to me, at least the ones with whom I was acquainted.

All of this changed following a minister's conference where I received a very detailed prophecy. One of the first things prophesied was, "The substance of thy house (Christian

Chapel) shall flourish in this year of 1982. You will have this breakthrough, sayeth the Lord your God."

At that time, Christian Chapel was a small congregation of less than two hundred members. We did not have a building, so we were worshiping in the Thoreau Junior High Building in Tulsa, Oklahoma. We desperately needed our own facilities, but we lacked the funds to buy property or to build. Seven months after I received that prophetic word, Christian Chapel received an unexpected donation of $439,444.79. That was nearly double our annual income. The substance of our house was flourishing!

It was also prophesied that I would preach before the leaders of my denomination and before influential people around the world. I must say, that was a stretch for me. I was a relatively unknown pastor who had spent his entire ministry serving small congregations in obscure places. But within six weeks, I received an invitation to be one of the speakers at the biannual convention of the International Correspondence Institute in Brussels, Belgium. Missionary delegates came from around the world, and Dr. George Flattery, the president and founder of ICI, as well as J. Philip Hogan, the director of foreign missions for the Assemblies of God, were both in attendance.

A few weeks later, I received an invitation to preach at the General Council for the Argentine Assemblies of God in Buenos Aires, Argentina. Of course, the general superintendent of the Argentine Assemblies of God was present. Shortly thereafter, I was invited to preach at the Southern Cone missionary retreat. Loren Triplett, the regional director for Assemblies of God missions in Latin America, was in attendance, and once again, I was speaking before the leaders of my denomination. Needless to say, my skepticism regarding prophecy was fading.

Let me share one more word from that prophecy: "My son, I will never fail to put a word in your mouth. Truly, this is My covenant with you. In that very hour you will give a word that will cause you to stumble backward, and you will put your hand on your mouth and say, 'Have I said this?' And the Lord will say, 'No, I said it through you.'"

That particular prophecy has been fulfilled any number of times. For instance, I prayed for a young couple who were unable to have children. After spending thousands of dollars, and undergoing a myriad of medical tests, the doctors informed them that their situation was hopeless. In desperation, they came for prayer, and I prayed for them. As they turned to walk away, the Holy Spirit came upon me, and I suddenly blurted out,

"The Lord says that about this time next year you will have a son!"

I literally stumbled backward and put my hand over my mouth. I couldn't believe I had said that—and in front of hundreds of people! I couldn't help wondering if I had given them false hope and had made a fool of myself in the process.

I need not have worried. One year later, that woman gave birth to a healthy baby boy just as the Lord had promised!

So, what should you do if you receive a personal prophecy? First Corinthians 14:29 instructs us to carefully consider what was prophesied. First, you measure it against the Scriptures to see if it lines up with the Word of God. I call this the "Word test." If it is contrary to the Scriptures in any way, you must reject it. If it passes the Word test, then ask yourself if the prophecy edifies you—does it strengthen you, encourage you, and/or comfort you (see 1 Corinthians 14:3)? Finally, you should ask other spiritually mature believers if they feel it is valid (1 Corinthians 14:29).

Although the Holy Spirit can speak through anyone at any time—He even spoke through Balaam's donkey (Numbers 22:28)—I put more confidence in a prophecy when a spiritually mature and emotionally whole person gives it. Not infrequently, zealous but spiritually immature people prophesy out of their own emotions. Jeremiah 23:16 says, "They speak visions from their own minds, not from the mouth of the Lord." Deuteronomy 18:22 puts it this way: "That prophet has spoken presumptuously." That is, he has spoken out of his own emotions rather than by the inspiration of the Holy Spirit.

If the prophecy you have received is based on misguided zeal or emotion, set it aside. Over time, it will simply fade away.

"If what a prophet proclaims in the name of the LORD does not take place or come true, that is a message the LORD has not spoken" (Deuteronomy 18:22).

A final word of caution: Do not attempt to make a prophecy come to pass. If it is truly from the Lord, He will bring it to pass. If it is not from the Lord, trying to force it will only create a mess. Pray over it, meditate upon it, but leave it in the Lord's hands.

I am no one special, yet the Lord has spoken to me again and again in any number of different ways. Daily He speaks to me from His Word—teaching me, correcting me, guiding me, and comforting me. It is far and away the most common way He speaks. He also speaks through "feelings" that become thoughts and impressions that direct my steps. On occasion, He speaks through the wisdom and counsel of godly people. A less common way He speaks is through dreams, visions, and prophecies. **If He is speaking to me, I can assure you He is speaking to you.** Therefore, let us respond as the boy Samuel did: "Speak, for your servant is listening" (1 Samuel 3:10).

If you sincerely desire to hear God's voice, pray this prayer with me. "Lord, give me ears to hear Your voice, a heart to receive Your Word, a will to obey, and the faith to act. In Your holy name I pray. Amen."

If you would like to receive Jesus Christ as your personal Savior please pray this prayer.

Father God, I believe that Jesus is Your only begotten Son. I believe He became a man and lived a sinless life. I believe He died on the cross as punishment for my sins. I believe you raised Him from the dead and that He is now seated at Your right hand making intercession for us.

I confess that I am a sinner. I have transgressed Your holy law. I have sinned against You and those I love. I cannot save myself. I cannot undo the wrong I have done. Jesus is my only hope.

Lord Jesus, forgive my sins. By faith I receive You as my Lord and my savior. Because You were made to be sin for me I am being made righteous. Because You bore the shame of the cross I do not have to bear the shame of my sin. Because You died and rose again I am saved. In Your holy name I pray. Amen

If you prayed this prayer to receive Jesus as your Savior I would love to hear from you. Please contact me at:

Richard Exley Ministries
pastorrichardexley@gmail.com

ENDNOTES

1   David Wilkerson, *I'm Not Mad at God* (Minneapolis: Bethany Fellowship, 1967), 32

2   Hannah Whitall Smith, *The Christian's Secret of a Happy Life*, quoted in *Disciplines for the Inner Life* by Bob Benson and Michael W. Benson (Waco: Word Books, 1985), 183.

3   Visions: Genesis 15:1–2; 46:2; Numbers 12:6; 1 Samuel 3:1; 1 Kings 22:17; Psalm 89:19; Isaiah 1:1; Jeremiah 24:1; Ezekiel 1:1; Daniel 1:17; 2:19; 7:13; Acts 9:10–17; 10:1–22; 16:9–10; 18:9–11; 22:17–18; Hebrews 1:1; Revelation 1:1, 9; 4:1; 5:11; 9:15–19; 13:1; 17:18; 21:10.

4   Personal prophecy: 1 Samuel 10:1–9; 1 Kings 20:35–43; 1 Kings 21:17; Acts 15:32, 21:8–11.

Richard Exley is a man with a rich diversity of experiences. He has been a pastor, conference and retreat speaker, as well as a radio broadcaster. In addition, he has written more than thirty books. He loves spending time with his wife, Brenda Starr, in their secluded cabin overlooking picturesque Beaver Lake. He enjoys quiet talks with old friends, kerosene lamps, good books, a warm fire when it's cold, and a good cup of coffee anytime.

You may contact the author at
pastorrichardexley@gmail.com.

BOOKS BY RICHARD EXLEY

Dancing in the Dark
Deliver Me
Encounters at the Cross
Encounters with Christ
From Grief to Gratefulness
Intimate Moments for Couples
Man of Valor
One-Minute Devotion
Perils of Power
Storm Shelter—A Refuge in Turbulent Times
Strength for the Storm
The Alabaster Cross (Novel)
The Letter (Novel)
The Making of a Man
The Gift of Gratitude
When You Lose Someone You Love
When Your World's Falling Apart

www.RichardExleyBooks.com